TEXAS HISTORY STORIES

HOUSTON, AUSTIN, CROCKETT, LA SALLE

FOR SUPPLEMENTARY READING
IN PRIMARY GRADES

E. G. LITTLEJOHN

Published by Left of Brain Books

Copyright © 2021 Left of Brain Books

ISBN 978-1-396-31919-8

First Edition

All rights reserved. No part of this publication may be reproduced, distributed, or transmitted in any form or by any means, including photocopying, recording, or other electronic or mechanical methods, without the prior written permission of the publisher, except in the case of brief quotations embodied in critical reviews and certain other noncommercial uses permitted by copyright law. Left of Brain Books is a division of Left Of Brain Onboarding Pty Ltd.

Table of Contents

SAM HOUSTON	1
STEPHEN F. AUSTIN	7
DAVID CROCKETT	12
LA SALLE	20

SAM HOUSTON

Sam Houston was born in Vir-gin-ia.
His parents were poor people.
He had five brothers and three sisters.
When Sam was eight years old he started to school.
There were few good schools in Vir-gin-ia in those days.
There were no free schools, such as we have to-day.
Sam could go to school only late in the winter.
The rest of the year he was kept at hard work.
Sometimes, if he worked well, he was allowed to run home from the fields, to be in time to take his place in spelling.
He learned to read and write and cipher.
When he was thirteen years old, he had gone to school but six months in all.
It was then that his father died. After the death of his father, his mother sold the old home in Vir-gin-ia and took her fam-i-ly across the mountains into Ten-nes-see.

At that time Ten-nes-see was only a great wilderness. Indians were everywhere. There were dense forests full of wolves, bears and other wild animals.

The little party halted eight miles from the Ten-nes-see River, which was the boundary between the white men and the Cherokee Indians. Here a new log cabin was built and a farm cleared

Sam was set to work on the farm with his brothers. But he liked hunting and fishing better than work. He soon became ac-quaint-ed with the Indians living near his home and spent much of his time with them in the woods.

His fam-i-ly did not like this, so he was put to work in a country store. Sam had no greater liking for this kind of life than for farming, so one day he sudden-ly dis-ap-pear-ed. A great search was made for him, but he could not be found for several weeks.

At last it was learned that he had gone back to his friends, the Indians.

When asked why he had acted in this way, he said because he liked to measure deer tracks better than tape.

When his clothes were worn out, he returned home for more.

He was kindly received by his mother, who gave him all the clothes he needed.

But he could not forget his free life in the woods.

He longed to sport with the happy Indian boys.

He longed to chase the deer.

He longed for the fresh air of the forests.

And he was soon back among the Indians again. He staid with them most of the time, till he was eighteen years of age.

Sam did not like hard study, but he was very fond of reading.

His favorite book was Homer's Iliad, which he carried with him to the woods.

This he read by the light of the Indians' campfire at night, and in the daytime, when the chase was ended, he would lay himself down under the shade of a great tree and read for hours at a time.

When he was eighteen years old, he left the Indians and began to teach school for the pale faces, as the whites were called.

He wanted money to pay some debts. He had few pupils at first, but he was not one of the kind that gives up easily. He kept right on and soon had more pupils than he could teach. For pay he received corn, cotton cloth and a little money.

When he had made enough money to pay his debts, he shut up his school.

He soon after became a soldier in the U-nit-ed States army.

When he marched away, his mother, standing in the door of her cottage, handed him his musket, saying "Here, my son, take this musket and never disgrace it for re-mem-ber, I had rather all my sons should fill one hon-or-a-ble grave than that one of them should turn his back to save his life. The door of my cottage is ever open to brave men, but always shut against cowards."

He never forgot his mother's words. Where the battle was thickest, there he was always to be found.

In a battle with the Indians he was shot by an arrow that struck deep into his thigh.

He tried to pull it out but failed. A comrade was then called upon to pull it out, but failed also. "Try again," said Houston, raising his sword, "and pull it out or I strike you, down." This time it came, tearing away the flesh and leaving an ugly wound, which never got entirely well.

When the war was over he was sent to New Or-le-ans.

This was a long way from his home. There were no railroads in those days, so he, with two other young men, floated down the Mississippi River in a canoe.

One day, as their skiff was turning a bend in the river, they saw a strange sight. It was a vessel coming up stream without any sails and sending up a heavy column of smoke.

They thought it must be on fire.

On coming closer, they saw it was a steam boat, the first that ever went up the Mississippi River.

He soon returned to Ten-nes-see and made his home in the city of Nashville.

He studied law and became a great lawyer. Before long people began to hear about him all over the State. The people wanted a wise man to go to Con-gress to help make laws for the whole land. When e-lec-tion day came they chose Sam Houston to go.

When his time was out, they chose him to go back again.

He did his work so well in Con-gress that people began to say that he would make a good Gov-ern-or of the State.

Sam Houston never neg-lect-ed his work. Whatever he had to do, he did well. And so he was chosen Gov-er-nor.

For some cause he soon gave up the Gov-ern-or ship and went to live again with his friends, the Cher-o-kee Indians.

The Indians were delighted to have him with them once more.

Years before he had been adopted as a son by the Cherokee chief.

He was given the name Col-o-neh, which means "the Rover."

When the old chief heard that his son was coming to see him once more, he went down to the river to meet him, taking his whole fam-i-ly with him.

When he landed, the old chief threw his arms around him and embraced him with great af-fec-tion.

The chief said to him: "My son, eleven winters have passed since we met.

"My heart has wandered often where you were.

"I heard you were a great chief among your people.

"We are in trouble, and the Great Spirit has sent you to tell us what to do and take the trouble away from us.

"I know you will be our friend, for our hearts are near to you.

"My wigwam is yours, my home is yours, my people are yours rest with us."

Houston was glad to be back again with his old friend.

He said that when he laid himself down to sleep that night he felt like a lost child returned at last to his father's house.

Houston was always the friend of the red man.

He said that in all the years he had known them he was never deceived by one of them.

Houston said the Indians were treated badly by the white man. He had taken their lands away from them.

He had robbed them of their forests and game.

He had given them "fire-wa-ter" to drink.

Houston loved them and felt sorry for them. He said he would do all he could to help them. He and they were children of the same Great Father.

He got them money for their lands. He would not let anyone sell them "fire-wa-ter." He had the bad men, who ill-treated them, punished.

After three years of forest life among the Indians, Houston determined to become a herdsman.

A herdsman is one who raises cattle.

The broad prairies of Texas are covered with grass which cattle like to eat.

Houston thought Texas would be a good place to start his ranch.

So, in 1832, with a few friends, he came to Texas. He stopped for a while at Nac-og-do-ches, and then went on to San An-to-ni-o.

At this time Texas belonged to Mex-i-co.

The people of Texas were badly treated by the Mex-i-cans.

Many of them were thrown into prison without cause.

They were not allowed to worship God in the way they wanted to.

They were not allowed to keep guns to protect themselves from the Indians.

They were given no public schools.
They were not allowed to make their own laws.
They were in great trouble and knew not what to do.
They thought Houston might be able to help them.
He was in-vit-ed to become their leader.

Houston was always careful about what he said and did, and the people felt safe while he was their leader.

War soon broke out between Texas and Mex-i-co, and Houston was made gen-er-al of the Texan army.

He was a wise com-mand-er.

He watched the enemy carefully.

When Gen-er-al San-ta Anna, the Mex-i-can com-mand-er, marched his army into Texas, Houston was on the lookout for him.

The two armies met on the banks of the San Ja-cin-to River, not far from the present city of Houston.

San-ta An-na's army was nearly three times as large as Houston's. Before going into battle, Houston made a speech to his men.

He told them that when they went into the fight to re-mem-ber the Al-a-mo.

The Al-a-mo is an old church in San An-ton-io. In this old church there had been a battle, in which one hundred and fifty brave Texans had been killed by the Mex-i-cans.

Houston wanted his men to re-mem-ber this, so they would pay the Mex-i-cans back.

The battle was fought April 21, 1836. It is called the Battle of San Jacinto.

The Texans rushed into the battle shouting "Re-mem-ber the Al-a-mo!" "Re-mem-ber the Al-a-mo!"

The Mex-i-cans were very much frightened and soon began to run.

The Texans followed them, killing many of them. Gen-er-al San-ta An-na was taken pris-on-er. He was found the day after the battle crawling on all fours through the tall grass of the prairie. He had found some old clothes, which he put on so that no one would know him. He was placed on a horse behind a soldier, who carried him to Gen-er-al Houston.

Houston's horse had been shot under him and he himself was badly wounded in the ankle. The wound was very painful and kept him awake all night. When San-ta An-na was brought to him he was lying on a pallet under an old oak tree and had fallen into a doze.

San-ta An-na told him who he was and begged that his life might be spared.

Houston was a brave man and he felt sorry for the prisoner. He asked San-ta An-na not to fight against the Texans any more, and then sent him back to his home in Mex-i-co.

Texas was now free from Mex-i-co. They could go back to their homes and live in peace. They could make their own laws.

The people now wanted someone for Pres-i-dent, and ev-er-y-bod-y thought Houston just the man for the place. He was e-lec-ted and served for two years.

Some years af-ter-wards he was made Pres-i-dent again, and then Gov-ern-or of the State of Texas.

When his time as Gov-ern-or was out, he went back to his home in Hunts-ville, Texas.

Here he lived a quiet and happy life with his wife and children.

He died July 26, 1863, aged seventy years. The whole people of Texas mourned for him as if he had been their father.

He is buried at Hunts-ville, Texas.

STEPHEN F. AUSTIN

Stephen F. Austin, like Houston, was a na-tive of Vir-gin-ia.
He was born No-vem-ber 3, 1793.
His father was Moses Austin.
He had one brother and one sister.
When Stephen was six years old his father moved with his fam-i-ly to Mis-sou-ri to mine for lead.

There were few white people in Mis-sou-ri at that time. Wild Indians roamed over the plains and hunted the buf-fa-lo. Sometimes they would suddenly appear before the white man's cabin, when the father was away, and carry off the mother and children. You may read in your history how Daniel Boone's daughter, and Mrs. Austin and her fam-i-ly were thus carried away.

Little Stephen had often seen the Indians gal-lop-ing over the prai-ries, and more than once he had heard their ter-ri-ble war-whoop.

There were no good schools in Mis-sou-ri at that time, so at the age of eleven Stephen was sent to school to Con-nec-ti-cut, his father's old home. He made good use of his time, and after four years he was able to enter a col-lege in Ken-tuck-y. He grad-u-a-ted from here in a short time with much honor.

When his school days were over he went back to Mis-sou-ri. He was kind and gentle in disposition. He was polite and respectful in his manners. He was a hard worker.

He soon won the good will of his neighbors and they sent him to the leg-is-lat-ure to help make the laws. They were so well pleased with him that they sent him back again and again for six years.

Austin now moved from Mis-sou-ri to Ark-an-sas and opened up a farm. His good name followed him, and the people here soon learned to love and trust him as those at his old home had done. In less than a year he was e-lect-ed judge.

About this time his father, Moses Austin went to San An-to-ni-o, Texas, to get permission to make a set-tle-ment in that country and to raise cotton and sugar. On his way he stopped at Stephen F. Austin's farm and asked him to help in making the settlement.

Stephen gave up his farm and went to New Or-le-ans to get col-o-nists for the new set-tle-ment.

When Moses Austin reached San An-to-ni-o he was coldly received by the gov-ern-or and ordered to quit the country. He was about to do this when a friend of his, Bar-on de Bas-trop, begged him not to go, and promised to see the gov-ern-or for him. This he did, and in a few days Austin was on his way back to Mis-sou-ri feeling that his request would be granted.

Mis-sou-ri was a long way from Texas in those days. One may take the cars now and in a few hours go from one place to the other. Austin traveled on horseback. On the journey he was beset by many dangers. The wild Co-man-che Indians roamed over the plains and killed every white man they met. The weather was very cold. The creeks and rivers, swollen by heavy rains, had to be crossed by swimming or on rafts.

When he got home to Mis-sou-ri, his health was ruined, and in a little while he died. Just before he died he sent word to his son Stephen to carry out his plans.

True to his promise to his father, Stephen F. Austin set out for San An-to-ni-o to see the Mex-i-can gov-ern-or. His friend, Don E-ras-mo Se-guin, went with him. He was welcomed by the gov-ern-or, to whom he showed his plans. The gov-ern-or liked the plans, and Austin was given land on which to settle his col-o-nists.

After picking out the land he wanted, he went back to New Or-le-ans for his settlers. But first he sent over a boatload of food for the people, as there was nothing in the country for them to eat when they should get there. The boat landed the supplies at the mouth of the Bra-zos River and hid them in the bushes along the bank. It then returned to New Or-le-ans for another load.

Austin, with his settlers, reached the Bra-zos on New Year's Day, 1822. They found their pro-vis-ions had been stolen by the Indians. They thought the boat would return with more supplies, but she did not come. She never came. Nothing was ever heard of her again. It is thought that she was lost at sea with all on board. But the people did not give up at this bad news. They set to work felling the trees, building themselves log cabins, and laying off fields. When they were hungry the hunters were sent to the woods to kill game. Often the hunters never came back, but were found dead scalped by the Indians.

Austin having made the set-tle-ment, he thought it right that he should tell the Mex-i-can gov-ern-or about it. So he set out for San An-to-ni-o, leaving a man named Josiah Bell as leader of the col-o-nists. When he got to San An-to-ni-o, he was told that he must go on to the City of Mex-i-co, more than a thousand miles away. There was a new pres-i-dent of Mex-i-co, who, he was told, would take his land away from him if he did not go.

With only one com-pan-ion he set out on the long and dan-ger-ous journey. Most of the way they traveled on foot. The country through which they passed was full of Indians and robbers. When two days out from San An-to-ni-o they were attacked and robbed by a band of Co-man-che Indians. Austin and his friend now dressed as beggars to escape the notice of the robbers. At night they slept on the ground in the open air and their food was of the coarsest kind.

After thirty-six days they reached the City of Mex-i-co. Here ev-er-y-thing was in dis-or-der. Austin tried to see the pres-i-dent, but could not. He waited awhile and tried again, but with no better luck. But he did not give up. He waited on for a year, and at last got the pres-i-dent to agree not to take the lands away from his col-o-nists but to give them more.

With this good news for his people he went back home. Everyone was glad to see him. He was welcomed as a father.

While Austin was gone to Mex-i-co, many other people had come into the col-o-ny and had begun to build towns. One of them they named San Fe-li-pe de Aus-tin, in honor of Austin. For ten years Austin watched over and care-ful-ly tended the little col-o-ny.

He punished the Indians and drove them from the country.

He made wise laws.

The people were happy in their new homes.

But now trouble came upon them. They were ill treated by the Mex-i-cans.

They were made to pay very high taxes. Their friends in the U-nit-ed States were no longer allowed to settle in the col-o-ny.

Their guns were taken away from them so they could not protect themselves from the In-dians. Mex-i-can soldiers were sent into the country, who behaved in a very insulting manner to the people.

Some of the Texans were ar-rest-ed and thrown into prison.

The people sent a letter to the pres-i-dent of Mex-i-co, asking for their rights.

The bearer of this letter was Stephen F. Austin.

Austin had not for-got-ten his other journey to Mex-i-co and its trials. His feelings told him not to go again, but to stay at home and be happy on his farm. But duty called him to go and he obeyed.

Gen-er-al San-ta Anna was then pres-i-dent of Mex-i-co. He pre-tend-ed to be the friend of Texas. But when Austin got to the City of Mex-i-co he would not see him. He had no time to listen to such a little matter as a letter from the Texans. Austin tried to see him again and again, but failed.

Sick at heart over his failure, Austin started home. He had not gone far when he was ar-rest-ed by some Mex-i-can soldiers, taken back to the city and thrown into prison. Here he was kept for more than two years. Part of the time he was denied light, books, ink, pen and paper. His health was almost ruined.

In the darkness of his prison he thought of his beloved Texas and how he might do something for her should he ever be set free.

But perhaps he should die in prison. Who then would help her? These thoughts, he said, almost crazed him.

But at last he was allowed to return to his home. Great was the joy of his people when they saw him again.

Austin had been at home hardly a month when war broke out between Mex-i-co and Texas. Mex-i-can soldiers were sent to take away the arms of the Texans. The Texans would not give them up. They needed them to protect their homes from the Indians. They said they would die before they would give them up.

The first fight took place at Gon-za-les, Oc-to-ber 2, 1835. The Texans had a small cannon here which the Mex-i-cans were told to take. "Take it if you can," said the Texans, and fired it into the enemy's ranks. They used the little gun so well that the Mex-i-cans were soon whipped. Four of them were killed and many wounded. The Texans lost not a man.

And now someone was wanted to command the Texas army. All eyes turned toward Austin, and he was chosen. It was now Gen-er-al Austin. He marched against the enemy and whipped them in several fights.

The people of Texas were poor. They had no money, and the soldiers needed food and clothes. They must get help somewhere. It was de-cid-ed to send someone to the U-nit-ed States to ask for help. Austin was chosen to go. When he was told that he had been chosen, he said, I go on this mission from a sense of duty. It is a bad example for anyone to refuse the call of the people when the country is in dif-fi-cult-y. "I have been called to go, and I obey the call." He left the army in charge of Gen-er-al Edward Burleson.

When he got to the U-nit-ed States he made speeches everywhere. He told of the wrongs of the Texans. He told of their cruel treatment by the Mex-i-cans. He told how bravely they were fighting for lib-er-ty. He asked for money and men to help them.

The people of the U-nit-ed States heard him gladly. All over the country men shouldered their rifles and set out for Texas. Money was sent, too.

After much fighting, the Mex-i-cans were whipped, and Texas became free. Peace once more settled down on the country. The soldiers laid down their arms and went back to their homes. Gardens were planted and fields plowed, and the whole country soon blossomed like a rose.

Austin was happy. His people were free. They had their own pres-i-dent and made their own laws.

Gen-er-al Sam Houston was the pres-i-dent.

The pres-i-dent needed some helpers, and he asked Austin to be one of them. There was much work to be done, but work for Texas was ever a pleasure to Austin. His health was weak and he worked too hard. He was seized with a sudden illness of which he died in a few days. December 27, 1836.

He was only 43 years old when he died.

The news of his death brought sorrow to every house-hold.

"He was known and beloved by all. Every child of every col-o-nist was known to him, was eager to welcome him, and to be permitted to play upon his knee."

He was buried at Peach Point, on the Brazos River, near Col-um-bi-a.

He is called The Father of Texas.

The city of Austin is named for him.

David Crockett

In the "Life of Sam Houston" you were told of the brave men who died in the Al-a-mo, fighting for the freedom of Texas.

One of these men was David Crockett.

David Crockett was born in Ten-nes-see. He was born on the 17th of August, in the year 1786. He had five brothers and three sisters. His father was very poor and the fam-i-ly lived far back in the backwoods.

The house in which they lived was made of logs. The chinks between the logs were filled with clay. There were no windows in the house, and light and fresh air came in through the door or through the chinks in the wall. Small holes were made in the walls through which guns might be put to shoot at the Indians.

The country was full of Indians at that time. They were very trou-ble-some. They would hide themselves near the settler's cabin and shoot down anyone who came out of the door. Often they would attack the house, break down the door, and kill the entire fam-i-ly. Crockett's grand-fa-ther and grand-mo-ther were both killed by them.

When David was seven or eight years old, his father gave up the farm and opened a mill. It was a mill for grinding corn into meal. The mill house was built on the banks of a small stream. One night there came a great rain storm. The water in the stream rose very high and washed away the mill house. It came up into the house in which Mr. Crockett lived and he had to move his fam-i-ly out to keep them from being drowned.

Mr. Crockett now moved to an-oth-er part of the country and opened a tavern.

David, being next to the oldest son, was a great help to his father and mother.

When trav-el-ers would stop at the tavern for the night, David would help them to unhitch and feed their teams.

One night an old Dutch-man by the name of Jacob Siler stopped at the tavern. He was going to Vir-gin-ia and had a large stock of cattle that he was taking with him. He wanted someone to help him with his cattle. He liked David's bright face and bus-i-ness manner, and asked Mr. Crockett to hire him. David was now about twelve years old. He loved his father and mother dearly and hated very much to leave home. But the fam-i-ly was very poor and he must help make the living. With a heavy heart he set out on the journey. It was four hundred miles to the place he was going and he had to travel on foot. He got very tired and often wished to be back at home with his dear father and mother. But he felt it his duty to go on.

His Dutch master was pleased with him and at the end of the journey gave him five or six dollars as his wages. It was a small sum, but David was very proud of it. It was the first money he had ever earned.

He wanted to go home and take the money to his father. But his master did not want him to go and kept a strict watch over him. One day he and two other boys were playing by the road side, some distance from the house. There came along three wagons. They belonged to an old man who was going to Ten-nes-see and who knew David's father. David begged the old man to take him home. The old man said he would stay that night at a tavern seven miles away, and if David could get there before day the next morning he would take him home. This was Sunday evening. David went back to his master's house and found the fam-i-ly were out on a visit. He gathered his clothes and his money and put them all to-geth-er under the head of his bed. He went to bed early that night, but he could not sleep. He kept thinking and thinking about his father and mother. And then, too, what if his master should find out that he was going home?

About three hours before day he got up to make his start. The night was dark and cold. It was snowing fast, and the snow was then on the ground about eight inches deep. Before he got to the wagons it was up to his knees.

He got to the wagons about an hour before day. The men were al-read-y up and getting ready to start. The old man treated him with great kindness. David warmed himself by the fire and ate a hearty break-fast, after which the party set out on their journey.

How slowly the wheels turned round. To David they seemed almost to stop. It seemed to him that he would never get home. He thought he could go faster by walking, so he told his old friend good-bye and set out on foot. He walked on until he was ov-er-tak-en by a man leading a horse, who offered to let him ride. He was very glad of this chance, as he was very tired. This kind man took him within fifteen miles of his father's house, when they parted and David walked home.

Up to this time David had never been to school a day. He could neither read nor write. Near his father's house was a little country school, kept by a man named Kitchen. To this school his father now sent him.

He had gone but four days and had just begun to learn his letters, when a falling out with a boy much larger and older than himself caused him to quit school.

He did not go to school again until he was fif-teen years old. Then he began to think that all his troubles were caused by his want of learning, and that he had better go to school some more. By working two days a week he got one of his neighbors to board him, and went to school the other four days of the week. He kept this up for six months. In this time he had learned to read a little, to write his own name, and to cipher some. And this was all the schooling he ever had. David was very fond of shooting, and as soon as he could get money enough bought him a good rifle. He carried it with him wherever he went. He often went to shooting matches, where they shot for beef. He was such a good shot that he often won the whole beef.

When he grew to be a man he became a great hunter. The country where he lived was full of deer, bears and other wild an-i-mals. When his fam-i-ly wanted meat, he would go out into the woods and shoot a deer or a bear.

Here is a story he tells of one of his bear hunts: "In the morning I left my son at the camp, and we started towards the canebrake. When we had gone about a mile, we started a very large bear, but we had to go very slowly, as the earth was full of cracks, caused by earth quakes, and there was much danger of falling into them. We kept in hearing of the dogs, though, for about three miles, when we came to the cane-brake.

"By this time several of the dogs had got tired and come back. We went ahead for some little time into the cane-brake, when we met the bear coming straight to us, and not more than twenty yards off. I started my dogs after him, and I followed on to about the middle of the cane-brake. Here I found the bear in an old stump of a tree about twenty feet high, with the dogs barking all around him. When I got close enough to shoot, I fired, and the bear fell. I ran up to him, but he was not dead. I loaded my gun as quickly as I could, shot him again and killed him. When we had skinned the bear, we cut off the fat, packed it on our horses, and started back to camp. We had gone but a little way when I heard my dogs barking again. I jumped down from my horse and gave him to my friend. He went on to camp, and I followed the dogs with all my might.

"Soon night came on. The woods were rough and hilly and all covered over with cane. I had to move very slowly. Sev-e-ral times I fell over logs and into cracks made by the earth-quakes. I was very much afraid I would break my gun. I went on about three miles till I came to a big creek which I waded. The water was about knee-deep and very cold. It was now so very dark that I could hardly see my way. When I got to the dogs, I found they had treed a bear in a large forked tree.

"I could see the dark hump in the tree, but not well enough to shoot. I hunted for some dry brush to make a light, but could find none. At last I thought I could shoot by guess and kill him. I pointed as near the hump as I could and fired. The bear did not fall, but climbed higher and got out on a limb, where I could see him better. I loaded again and fired, but he didn't move at all. I was loading for a third fire, when, the first thing I knew, the bear was down among the dogs, and they were fighting all around me. At last the bear got into one of the cracks made by the earth-quakes. I could not see a wink. I pushed my gun against him and fired. With that he jumped out of the crack, and he and the dogs had another hard fight around me. At last the dogs forced him back into the crack again.

"I had laid down my gun in the dark, and I now began to hunt for it. I got hold of a pole, and I thought I would punch the bear awhile with that. When I punched him, the dog would jump in on him, when he would bite them and make them jump out again.

"While the dogs kept his head toward them, I got down into the crack and killed him with a long knife I carried in my belt.

"I suffered very much with cold that night. My clothes were wet and frozen. My fire was very bad and I could not find anything that would burn well to make it any better. I thought I should freeze if I didn't warm myself, in some way by ex-er-cise. I got up and shouted awhile with all my might. Then I would jump up and down and throw myself into all sorts of motions. But this would not do. My blood was getting cold and the chills were coming all over me. I was so tired, too, that I could hardly walk. But I thought I would do the best I could to save my life. I went to a tree about two feet through and not a limb on it for thirty feet, and I would climb up to the limbs, then lock my arms around it and slide don two the bottom again. I kept on doing this till daylight. In the morning I hung my bear up, so as to be safe, and set out to hunt for my camp. I found it in a short while. My son and my friend were rejoiced to see me, as they had given me up for lost."

Crockett was a great Indian fighter, as well as bear hunter. He was in many battles with the Indians and was a brave soldier. When he went to war he was called Col-o-nel Crockett.

Col-o-nel Crockett was much liked by his neighbors wherever he lived. He was kind hearted. He was full of fun. He was pleasant to everyone he met. He was honest. In all things he tried to do what was right. His motto was, "Be sure you are right, then go ahead."

The people wanted a man of this kind to help make the laws, and they chose Col-o-nel Crockett. They sent him first to the Leg-is-lat-ure of the State, and then to Con-gress.

He stayed in Con-gress sev-er-al years. When his time was out, he determined to go to Texas and help her against the Mex-i-cans.

It made him very sad to leave his home. He loved his wife, his children and his friends. He loved his home and country. He loved freedom. Texas was fighting for freedom and needed soldiers very much. So bidding farewell to home and friends, he set out for that strange land. On the way he was joined by two com-pan-ions. One day they were riding through the prai-ries when they heard a low rumbling noise like thunder. They stopped and listened. Nearer and louder grew the noise. They looked in the dir-ec-tion from which the sound came and saw a great cloud of dust rising over the prai-rie. They thought it must be a storm coming. The noise grew louder and louder. The cloud of dust became thicker and thicker. Their horses became very much frightened, so they ran and caught them and rode into a grove of trees nearby. They had just got under the trees when a great herd of buf-fa-lo came dashing by as swift as the wind. If the Col-o-nel and his friends had not ridden under the trees they would have been trampled to death.

Col-o-nel Crockett had long wanted a chance to hunt buf-fa-lo, and now here it was. He watched the herd for a few moments, then put spurs to his horse and followed them, leaving his friends behind him. He rode on as fast as his horse could carry him. But he could not keep up with the buf-fa-loes, which were soon lost to sight in the distance.

He now stopped to let his horse breathe and to think how he should get back to his friends and the road he had left. He looked around him on every side, but nothing was to be seen but the broad prai-rie. Not even an an-i-mal was in sight. Not a sound was to be heard. He was lost on the prai-rie.

Night came on and he began to look for a place of shelter. He found a large tree that had blown down and he thought he would sleep in its top. He climbed up among the branches, when he heard a low growl. He looked up to see what sort of a bed-fel-low he was to have, when he saw, not more than five or six steps away, a great Mex-i-can lion. With flashing eyes and grinning teeth he was just ready to spring upon the Col-o-nel. As quickly as he could Crockett raised his rifle to his shoulder and fired. The ball struck the lion on the fore head, but did not hurt him much. The next moment he sprang. He lighted on the ground close by Crockett, who struck him over the head with the barrel of his rifle. But he didn't mind that at all. Crockett now threw down his gun and drew his large hunting knife. The lion came at him again and seized him by the shoulder. Crockett's foot tripped in a vine and he fell to the ground with the lion on top of him. Crockett thought his last hour had come. His arm and leg were badly torn. He felt himself getting very weak. Gath-er-ing all his strength for a last blow he struck the lion with all his might in the neck. The lion let go his hold and in another moment rolled over on his side dead.

Crockett now went back to the tree to make his bed. He threw some moss on the ground, and over it spread his horse blanket. On this bed he lay down and, being very tired, soon fell fast asleep. He awoke at daybreak next morning. He was sore and stiff from his fight with the lion. He went for his horse, but it had run away during the night. What should he do, away off in this wild country, afoot and alone?

While he was thinking, a band of In-di-ans rode up and sur-round-ed him. They were friendly to the white men. The chief gave Crockett another horse and promised to take him back to his friends. The camp was reached that evening, when Crockett bade farewell to his kind friends, the In-di-ans, and they rode away.

Crockett's com-pan-ions were delighted to see him. The next day they reached the Al-a-mo.

The Al-a-mo was an old church in the city of San An-to-ni-o. The Texans had taken the town from the Mex-i-cans some time before and turned the old church into a fort. Col-o-nel William B. Travis, with one hundred and eighty soldiers, held the fort for the Texans. Col-o-nel Travis and his men were glad to see Crockett and his companions and welcomed them to the fort.

Not many days after Crockett's ar-riv-al news came that the Mex-i-can Gen-er-al, San-ta An-na with a large army was coming to take the fort.

The Texans made ready to receive them. They stored their arms and provisions in the fort and raised the Texas flag.

The Mex-i-cans marched into the city with a blood-red flag flying. This red flag meant that all who were taken pris-on-ers would be put to death.

They sent a mes-sen-ger to Col-o-nel Travis, asking him to sur-ren-der. They told him that if he did not sur-ren-der every man would be put to death. Col-o-nel Travis' answer was a cannon shot.

Col-o-nel Travis now sent word to Gen-er-al Houston that he was sur-round-ed by the Mex-i-cans and asked for help. In his letter he said, "I shall never sur-ren-der or retreat! Vic-to-ry or death!"

But no help came. The Mex-i-cans drew nearer and nearer to the fort. On the 6th of March, 1836, before daybreak, they closed about the walls of the fort. They brought ladders with them and tried to climb over the walls. But the Texans poured upon them a ter-ri-ble hail of shot and shell and kept them back. A second time they went up the ladders, but with no better success. A third time they swarmed up the ladders, driven by the swords of their of-fi-cers. This time they went over the walls amongst the Texans. The Texans "fought like brave men—long and well." They sold their lives as dearly as pos-si-ble. When daylight came only six of them were found alive. Among this number was Col-o-nel Crockett. He stood alone in a corner of the fort, the barrel of his shat-tered rifle in his right hand and his huge bowie knife in his left. There was a great gash across his forehead. Twenty or thirty of his foes lay dead at his feet.

Crockett with the other five Texans were taken pris-on-er and carried before Gen-er-al San-ta An-na, who ordered them to be put to death at once.

When Crockett heard this order he sprang like a tiger at San-ta An-na, but before he could reach him a dozen swords pierced his heart and he fell and died without a groan.

La Salle

The first white man to make a set-tle-ment in Texas was Robert Cav-e-lier de la Salle.

La Salle was a Frenchman.

He was born at Rou-en, Nor-man-dy, in 1643.

His father, who was a wealthy merchant, gave him a fine ed-u-ca-tion and in-tend-ed him to be a priest.

At this time thousands of Frenchmen were flocking to the New World in search of fortune. Won-der-ful stories were told of the land beyond the sea. There was the Fountain of Youth, that wondrous spring that would restore youth and beauty to all who bathed in its waters. There was El Do-ra-do, the golden land, where the people ate and drank out of vessels of silver and gold.

The boy, La Salle, heard these stories, and he longed for the time to come when he, too, should cross the waters and visit this new found land.

He could not study as he once did. The school room seemed a prison to him. Every day, as he heard these stories, he became more restless and dis-con-tent-ed. A life of bold ad-vent-ure was his only dream of hap-pi-ness.

At last, he gave up the idea of be-com-ing a priest, and at the age of twenty-four joined an ex-pe-di-tion to Can-a-da.

And now the, free life he had been longing for was his.

He went first to Mont-re-al, where he had a brother, a priest.

Mont-re-al was at that time a very dan-ger-ous place.

It was sur-round-ed by In-di-ans who were very savage land always at war with the people of the French col-o-ny. No one could venture out into the fields or forests without fear of losing his life.

Eight or nine miles from Mont-re-al, in the heart of the forest, La Salle bought some land and began to make a set-tle-ment. He built a strong fort for pro-tec-tion against the In-di-ans. The ground was cleared of trees and log cabins were built for the settlers.

The In-di-ans often came to the set-tle-ment to trade furs, beads and other trinkets of the white man, and for powder and shot.

One day he was vis-i-ted by a band of In-di-ans, who told him of a great river many miles to the west, flowing into the sea.

La Salle, like Co-lum-bus, wanted to find a short route to Chi-na. He thought he might get to Chi-na by sailing down this great river.

This thought set him on fire. Al-read-y he saw his ships anchored in the ports of Chi-na and loading with the precious stuffs which all the world wanted.

He could not rest. He went to the Gov-ern-or of Can-a-da to get per-mis-sion to sail down the great river.

Per-mis-sion was given, and La Salle set out on his journey to find the great Father of Waters.

Ten long years he spent in the wil-der-ness seeking for the great river. Through frozen forests and over trackless fields of snow he took his way, every step watched by a savage In-di-an.

Dangers beset him on every side. Sev-er-al times his en-e-mies tried to poison him. Often he was in danger of star-va-tion and drowning. His friends tried to persuade him to give up his search and, when he refused to do so, left him.

But nothing could turn him from his purpose. He would find the great river or die trying.

At last his patience was re-ward-ed. On the sixth of February, 1682, he paddled his canoes out upon the broad bosom of the Mis-sis-sip-pi.

For many days his canoes floated down the mighty stream. At one time they were in danger of being upset by large masses of floating ice. At another time the party was attacked by In-di-ans, who sent a shower of arrows whizzing round their heads.

On the sixth of April, two months from the time the journey had begun, La Salle and his party reached the mouth of the Mis-sis-sip-pi. Here La Salle set up a column and took possession of the country on both sides of the river for his king, Louis IV of France. La Salle called the name of the country Lou-is-i-an-a.

La Salle now returned to Can-a-da and from there to France to tell the king of his great dis-cov-er-y. He told of the mighty river down which he had floated, and of the beau-ti-ful country through which it flowed. He told of great fortunes which might be made there trading with the In-di-ans, and of the rich silver mines of Mex-i-co that might be taken from the Span-iards. He told of the poor heathen In-di-ans who might be made Christ-ians. He asked per-mis-sion of the king to make a set-tle-ment at the mouth of the river where he had set up the column.

The king listened to all he said with much at-ten-tion, and then told La Salle that his wish should be granted.

La Salle went to work at once to make ready for the voyage. His heart throbbed with hap-pi-ness, for this was his dream come true.

Soon four vessels were ready. Their names were Ai-ma-ble, Jo-li, Belle and St. Fran-cis.

On board these vessels were one hundred and eighty men, seven priests and seven fam-i-lies.

The Jo-li was a war ship carrying thirty-six guns, and on this La Salle sailed.

The voyage was begun July 24, 1684. The passage across the At-lan-tic was a long and stormy one. They had been out only four days when the Jo-li broke her bow-sprit and had to sail back to get it mended. A great storm sep-a-rat-ed the vessels, and the store-ship St. Francis was taken by the Span-iards. La Salle was attacked by a fever which almost cost him his life.

After sailing for two months they entered the Gulf of Mex-i-co. All eyes now kept a sharp lookout for the mouth of the Mis-sis-sip-pi, where La Salle intended to plant his col-o-ny.

Day after day passed by, but no signs of the great river were to be seen. At last a wide opening was seen between two low points of land. La Salle thought this was the Mis-sis-sip-pi, but it was Gal-ves-ton Bay.

La Salle had left one of his vessels behind and he waited here five or six days for it to come up. He then sailed westward along the Texas coast. He tried to land at sev-er-al places, but the sandbars and breakers kept him back. Some In-di-ans swam out through the surf and were taken on board.

Buf-fa-lo were seen running along the shore and deer grazed on the prairie.

The ships kept sailing to the west till Mat-a-gor-da Bay was reached. La Salle thought this was the Mis-sis-sip-pi and landed his men. One of his ships was wrecked when it crossed the bar.

La Salle was on the shore watching the ship. Some of his men were a short distance away cutting down a tree to make a canoe. Sud-den-ly some of them came running to La Salle crying out that their com-pan-ions had been carried away by the In-di-ans.

La Salle ordered his men to take their arms and pursue the In-di-ans. They soon found the In-di-an village and rescued the captives.

The whole party now camped on the beach. They had bad water and food which made many of them sick. Five or six died every day. The Indians came to the camp and stole blankets and other ar-ti-cles and killed several of the Frenchmen.

La Salle soon found that he was not on the Mis-sis-sip-pi. It was a great dis-ap-point-ment to him. But it must be found, cost what it might.

He built a fort, which he named Fort St. Louis, to protect his people from the In-di-ans, and then set out with fifty men to search for the Mis-sis-sip-pi.

For weeks and months they wandered through the wil-der-ness, but no glimpse of the river gladdened their eyes or lightened their hearts. They were attacked by the In-di-ans and many of their number killed. Their clothes were in rags. Food was scarce. At last, foot-sore and weary, they returned to the fort.

The dangers and dis-ap-point-ments through which he had passed made La Salle ill. For many days it was thought that he would die. He got well, however, and at once began to make ready for another journey to search for the river. This time he took twenty men with him, among whom were his brother and nephew, and journeyed in a north-east-er-ly di-rec-tion. It was a beau-ti-ful country through which he passed. The prai-ries were covered with lovely flowers and fresh green grass, on which thousands of buf-fa-lo were feeding.

But mis-for-tune and dis-ap-point-ment met him again and caused him to return to the fort. Only eight men returned with him. One had been lost and one devoured by an al-li-ga-tor, four de-sert-ed him, and the others, too weak to keep up, were left to die upon the prai-rie.

Of the one hundred and eighty col-o-nists only forty-five now remained.

But La Salle was not the man to give up. He knew no such word as fail. After a short rest he prepared to renew his search.

When ev-er-y-thing was ready, he called his little com-pa-ny about him and told them of his plans. Twenty men were to go with him and the others were to remain at the fort till he could bring them help. He told those who were to remain to be brave and patient and watch for his coming. Then he said farewell and rode out of the gate. "It was a bitter parting, one of sighs, tears and em-brac-ings." Slowly the little party wound its way along the prairie, till it was lost to sight in the distance.

In the party were two nephews and a brother of La Salle; the trusty soldier Jou-tel, and a priest An-as-tase Dou-av; Du-haut and Li-o-tot, the surgeon.

"They passed the prai-rie and neared the forest. Here they saw buf-fa-lo and the hunters killed sev-er-al of them. Heavy clouds gathered over them and it rained all night but they sheltered themselves under the hides of the buffalo they had killed."

They met In-di-ans almost every day. They often vis-i-ted them in their lodges and smoked with them the peace-pipe.

But now trouble arose among the party. Du-haut and Li-o-tot, the surgeon, hated La Salle and his nephew Mor-an-get, and had sworn ven-geance against them. Food was getting scarce in the camp, and La Salle sent a party of men ahead to find some corn and beans which he had hidden on one of his other journeys.

In this party were Du-haut, Li-o-tot, Ni-ka, an In-di-an hunter, and La Salle's servant, Sa-get. They found the food, but it was spoiled. On their way back to camp they saw buf-fa-lo, and Ni-ka killed two of them.

They cut up the meat and laid it on scaffolds for smoking and sent word to La Salle to send horses for it. Next morning La Salle sent Mor-an-get and another man with horses for the meat. When they arrived at the hunter's camp Mor-an-get and Du-haut began to quarrel about the meat.

That night, Mor-an-get, Ni-ka and Sa-get were killed while they slept. All the next day La Salle watched for their return. When they did not come, he resolved to go and look for them. He did not know the way, and he told an In-di-an that he would give him a hatchet to guide him.

La Salle was very sad and down-heart-ed, and seemed to feel that something was wrong. In the morning he set out with his In-di-an guide and Father An-as-tase.

When close to Du-haut's camp he fired his gun to let his men know where he was.

Du-haut heard the gun and guessed rightly that it was La Salle coming to look for his nephew. He and the surgeon, Li-o-tot, crouched down in the long, dry, reed-like grass and waited for La Salle to come up.

When he came within speaking distance a shot was fired from the grass, quickly followed by another, and, pierced through the brain, La Salle dropped dead.

His body was dragged into the bushes and left a prey to the buzzards and the wolves.

Thus, age of forty-three died Robert Cav-e-lier de la Salle, one of the greatest men time, and one whom every Texan should delight to honor.

www.ingramcontent.com/pod-product-compliance
Lightning Source LLC
Chambersburg PA
CBHW020432010526
44118CB00010B/541